LEARNING THROUGH DISAGREEMENT

LEARNING THROUGH DISAGREEMENT

A Workbook for the Ethics of Business

MARVIN T. BROWN

broadview press

LIBRARY AND ARCHIVES CANADA CATALOGUING IN PUBLICATION

Brown, Marvin T., 1943-, author
    Learning through disagreement : a workbook for the ethics of business / Marvin T. Brown.

ISBN 978-1-55481-217-2 (pbk.)

    1. Conflict management—Study and teaching—Activity programs. 2. Business ethics—Study and teaching—Activity programs. I. Title.

HD42.B76 2014   658.4'053076   C2014-902118-6

BROADVIEW PRESS is an independent, international publishing house, incorporated in 1985.

We welcome comments and suggestions regarding any aspect of our publications—please feel free to contact us at the addresses below or at broadview@broadviewpress.com.

NORTH AMERICA
Post Office Box 1243
Peterborough, Ontario
K9J 7H5, Canada

customerservice@broadviewpress.com

555 Riverwalk Parkway
Tonawanda, NY 14150, USA
TEL: (705) 743–8990
FAX: (705) 743–8353

UK, EUROPE, CENTRAL ASIA, MIDDLE EAST, AFRICA, INDIA, AND SOUTHEAST ASIA
Eurospan Group, 3 Henrietta St., London WC2E 8LU, United Kingdom
TEL: 44 (0) 1767 604972 FAX: 44 (0) 1767 601640
eurospan@turpin-distribution.com

AUSTRALIA AND NEW ZEALAND
NewSouth Books
c/o TL Distribution, 15–23 Helles Ave.
Moorebank, NSW 2170, Australia
TEL: (02) 8778 9999 FAX: (02) 8778 9944
orders@tldistribution.com.au

www.broadviewpress.com

Edited by Martin Boyne
Typesetting by Em Dash Design

Printed in Canada

CONTENTS

Preface: About this Workbook   7

Introduction   9

CHAPTER ONE: A Dialogical Approach   13

    WORKSHEET 1-1: Dialogical Capacity   15

    WORKSHEET 1-2: Engaging in Dialogue   17

CHAPTER TWO: Resources for Making Better Decisions   19

    TABLE 2.1: Resources for Making Decisions   20

    Identifying Resources for Making Decisions   24

    TABLE 2.2: Steps Involved in Sharing Resources   25

    Creating Valid Syllogisms   26

    Exploring Assumptions   28

    TABLE 2.3: Sample Argument   30

    WORKSHEET 2-1: Sorting Out Different Resources   33

    WORKSHEET 2-2: Discovering Implicit Value Judgments   35

    WORKSHEET 2-3: Developing Valid Syllogisms   37

    WORKSHEET 2-4: Assumptions about Ourselves   39

    WORKSHEET 2-5: Uncovering Assumptions   41

    WORKSHEET 2-6: Discovering the Resources of
        Alternative Views   43

CHAPTER THREE: Engaging in an Ethical Analysis of Human Action   45

The Visionary, the Judge, and the Assessor   46

The Ethics of Purpose   47

The Ethics of Principle   49

TABLE 3.1: Principles of Distributive Justice   52

The Ethics of Consequence   52

Applying an Ethics of Purpose   55

Applying an Ethics of Principle   55

Applying an Ethics of Consequence   56

Developing the Modified Proposal   56

WORKSHEET 3-1: Applying an Ethics of Purpose   59

WORKSHEET 3-2: Applying an Ethics of Principle   61

WORKSHEET 3-3: Applying an Ethics of Consequence   63

CHAPTER FOUR: Doing the Work   65

Working Offline   65

Working Online   66

Developing Argumentative Dialogues   67

A Sample Argumentative Dialogue on Worker Cooperatives   68

Worksheet 4-1: An Outline for Your Argumentative Dialogues   77

Glossary   79

PREFACE:
ABOUT THIS WORKBOOK

When I started teaching ethics, I wanted to give students the skills and tools to explore and evaluate their opinions rather than only listen to mine. For students to learn how to actually do ethics, I thought they needed to learn how to analyze the reasons for different opinions and to evaluate them with different ethical standards. This workbook provides a structure for engaging in these activities. It is designed as a supplementary text for applied ethics courses and workshops that deal with controversial issues.

This workbook begins with a request: choose to engage in dialogue rather than debate. This does not require us to soften our stance toward controversial issues. It does require that we soften our stance toward one another. To engage in dialogue, people need to join together in seeking the best course of action when we all think we are right. Once we make this choice, the process itself enables us to understand the merits of other people's views, as well as our own.

Over the years, I have used this method in classes in business ethics, social ethics, and courses in communication. I have also used it in workshops for businesses, public agencies, and non-profit organizations. I see it now as a reliable format for developing good conversations on the difficult choices we face today. I hope you will find it useful in your work.

Marvin Brown

INTRODUCTION

Ethics begins with a question: "What should we do?" Most of the time, of course, we know what to do. Most of us simply do what we think is right, considering the world we think we live in. Only when someone disagrees with us, or we disagree with ourselves, do we face the question about the right thing to do. Disagreement, in other words, is necessary for ethics, and at the same time, ethics is necessary to deal with disagreements about what we should do.

In many cases, disagreement challenges our expectations. When you disagree with me, if I am on my toes, I might ask you why you disagree. More than likely, I will think that you do not know what I know. After all, if you knew what I knew, wouldn't we agree? It turns out that's not the case. Disagreement is not a sign of smarts, but a sign of different perceptions, experiences, values, and ways of being in the world.

Being different, of course, is not a problem by itself. If I am Christian and you are Muslim or an atheist, we do not need to disagree. We can simply share our religious beliefs and learn from each other. We can value and learn from our differences, without necessarily disagreeing about anything. But when we need to make a joint decision, our differences may cause disagreement.

You may think that fathers should select the education for their daughters, for example, and I may think that daughters should choose for themselves. This may be a religious and cultural difference. If we must decide whether or not to support equal education for boys and girls, not only might we have different views about the relationship between fathers and daughters, but we might also disagree about educational policies. What should we do when we disagree? This workbook offers a dialogical approach that honors different views and at the same time fosters mutual learning so that all parties can work together toward the best resolution of their disagreement.

Not all disagreements can be resolved, but they can be understood and evaluated. The dialogical approach presented here enables us to engage in such a process. To understand one another, we need to ask questions of inquiry. This is a mutual process that involves listening to each other for information and ideas that are different from the information and ideas behind our positions.

Once we understand the reasons for different positions, we can then begin the process of evaluating these positions by applying ethical approaches. Here we will use three approaches: an ethics of purpose, or what is called *teleology*; an ethics of principle, which is also called *deontology*; and an ethics of consequence, or *utilitarianism*. Each approach asks a different question. An ethics of purpose asks about the good end (i.e., purpose) that one is aiming for, and whether or not an action promotes that purpose. For example, a student might aim for an excellent grade in class and therefore decide to study during the weekend. An ethics of principle asks whether one could accept others acting in a similar way in similar circumstances. A student might refuse to cheat on an exam, for instance, because if everyone cheated the results would be worthless. An ethics of consequence asks about the impact of one's action on others and on oneself. For example, a student might decide not to speak up when someone is being bullied, because it would not do any good and could have negative consequences for all involved. More about these approaches later.

Each approach supplies normative standards for evaluating different proposed courses of action. The reason for three ethical approaches is that each one has some strengths and some weaknesses, so when taken together they help us reach a balanced assessment of the merits of different arguments. This process does not always end in agreement, but it does help us to understand different answers better—even our own—and to engage in a dialogical process that will promote good relationships and good decisions.

CHAPTER ONE

A DIALOGICAL APPROACH

When someone disagrees with us, most of us respond by either defending our own position or attacking the other person's, if we respond at all. In other words, we begin to debate the merits of different views. Such debates have their place, but in many cases they actually prevent a group or community from learning from each other and working together to make the best decision possible.

A dialogical approach offers a different response to disagreement. It proposes that we take disagreement as a sign that different people have different resources for understanding issues—different observations, values, and assumptions—and that if we could share them, we could make better decisions and develop better human relationships.

Dialogue begins with inquiry. To prevent disagreement from becoming a debate rather than a dialogue, we need to ask questions: "Why do you think that?" "What do you see here that I don't see?" Such questions begin a process of mutual sharing and learning. In some cases, asking such questions involves too much risk, because we do not know how others will respond. Dialogue, in other words, depends on believing that participants will be treated with respect.

A good dialogue has most of the following characteristics:

1. Participants feel safe enough to risk sharing their different points of view.
2. They ask questions in an effort to understand each other.

3.   They develop reasons for their views that others can understand and potentially accept.

4.   They trust each other's good intentions.

5.   They value their differences.

6.   They work together for the best solution possible.

You can use the exercise in Worksheet 1-1 (see p. 15) to assess your experiences and knowledge of engaging in dialogue.

After you finish the exercise, reflect on why you gave some individuals different numbers than others. Also, imagine how your conversation partners might use this exercise to assess their capacity for dialogue with you, and also with other people. If you think they also would have had some high numbers with some people, then all of you actually have the individual capacity for dialogue. Even if a person does not regularly engage in genuine dialogue with you, they may with others. The question is how to invite each other into the process of dialogue, so everyone can participate at their highest potential.

As noted earlier, ethics begins with questions: questions about what we should do. There is also a question about how we should decide what we should do when we disagree: should we engage in dialogue or debate? If we remember the goal, which is to make better decisions, then the obvious choice will be dialogue, because dialogue allows us to share our resources, and to learn from each other.

Worksheet 1-2 (see p. 17) provides an opportunity to engage in dialogue with another person. It begins with inquiry, listening, and appreciation of differences.

WORKSHEET 1-1   DIALOGICAL CAPACITY

List seven people with whom you regularly have conversations, and then rank them in terms of how often (1 = never, 5 = always) the conversations include these six features of dialogues:

FS = Feel safe

AQ = Ask questions

GR = Develop good reasons

TI = Trust each other's good intentions

VD = Value differences

WT = Work together

Seven people I talk with:	FS	AQ	GR	TI	VD	WT

WORKSHEET 1-2   ENGAGING IN DIALOGUE

List three things your partner knows that you do not.

1 ....

  ....

2 ....

  ....

3 ....

  ....

Ask questions to learn more about the three things listed above.

....

....

....

....

....

....

....

....

....

....

Share your partner's knowledge with the larger group.

CHAPTER TWO

RESOURCES FOR MAKING BETTER DECISIONS

The dialogical process of working though disagreement assumes that people have taken different positions on controversial issues. In most cases, the people holding these diverse positions all say they are right. So the conflict is between two (or more) beliefs about what's right, rather than a conflict between right and wrong. As we learned in the previous chapter, to turn disagreement into a process of learning we need to move toward dialogue, where each participant inquires about the reasons behind the different positions. To do a complete search, they will need to sort out the resources we draw on in making decisions, which include proposals, observations, value judgments, and assumptions.

These resources are closely interrelated. Our proposals depend on our observations of the situation, the values we believe in, and our assumptions about how things go together and how the world works. So if we select different observations, values, and assumptions, it makes sense that we will have different proposals. The triad of proposal, observation, and value can be seen as an argument for a position, with the observation and value supporting the proposal. Assumptions, on the other hand, provide the background that our arguments rely on. Once we understand the premises of each other's arguments, and their underlying assumptions, we can better understand why we disagree. Table 2.1 describes key differences among these four resources:

TABLE 2.1: RESOURCES FOR MAKING DECISIONS	
Proposals	Suggest actions—specific normative (should) statements
Observations	Describe situations—descriptive factual statements
Value Judgments	Guide actions—general normative statements
Assumptions	Provide background or context for positions—descriptive statements that express worldviews

Let's see how this works with the question of whether members of work teams or a work team's supervisor should decide how the team will get its work done. People disagree. Some say that teams should decide and some say they should not. So why do they disagree? To find out, we need to discover their different observations, value judgments, and assumptions.

Different observations reveal different perceptions of what facts are relevant for a particular proposal. A proposal that team members, rather than their supervisors, should decide how to get their work done could be supported by the observation that teams that have had such power have been more productive. Someone who disagrees with this proposal could observe that it is also true that sometimes giving team members such power leads to divisiveness and disrupts group harmony. Now, these different observations can be taken as barriers to deciding what to do, or they can be taken as additions to one's knowledge about working with and in teams. If we see them as an increase in a group's knowledge, then we already know more than we knew before, which can lead to an appreciation of each person's contribution. Appreciating different observations, of course, does not resolve our disagreement but rather furthers our inquiry. Why did the people making these arguments select different observations to support their different proposals? Part of the answer is implicit in the relationship between observations and proposals: a relationship that relies on our values.

Values are things that we hold dear, that matter to us. They include everything from fairness to compassion to efficiency, to list just a few. People may also value honor, wealth, or fame. In fact, we all have different values, and in different situations we affirm some and in other situations we affirm others. Here, however, we are using the idea of a value judgment in a more limited way. For example, if we return to the proposal that teams should decide how to get their work done because they will then be more productive, the value judgment is already implicit in our argument. As you might guess, the value judgment is this: "We should promote high productivity." The logic is quite simple: the proposal is a conclusion one has come to and the observation is a reason that supports it. The value judgment is a second reason implied in the connection between the proposal and the observation. A complete argument always has two reasons—observation and value judgment—to support a conclusion. More about this later.

The opposing proposal also has its particular value judgment: If that proposal is "We should not allow teams to decide how to get their work done, because it will disrupt a team's harmony," then the implicit value judgment would be "We should not disrupt a team's harmony." So we have two values now: productivity and harmony. Both are important for a well-functioning team, which means that once again, as with our observations, we have increased our pool of knowledge that we can use in deciding what we should do. We are learning from each other by appreciating our selection of different observations and value judgments. We can also use this increased knowledge about our different positions to explore the different worldviews, or different assumptions, from which they were developed.

So what are assumptions? The following exchange between Alan Greenspan, the former chairman of the US Federal Reserve Board, and Congressman Henry A. Waxman, in a 2008 congressional hearing, provides a good illustration of how we will use the notion of an assumption in this workbook.

> WAXMAN: This is your statement [quoting from Greenspan]—
> "I do have an ideology. My judgment is that free, competitive markets are by far the unrivalled way to organize economies. We have tried regulation, none meaningfully worked." That was your quote. You had the authority to prevent irresponsible lending practices that led to the sub-prime mortgage crisis. You were advised to do so by many others. And now the whole economy is paying the price. Do you feel that your ideology pushed you to make decisions you wish you had not made?

> GREENSPAN: ....[W]hat I am saying to you is, yes, I found a flaw. I don't know how significant or permanent it is, but I have been very distressed by that fact.

> WAXMAN: You found a flaw.

> GREENSPAN: I found a flaw in the model I perceived is the critical functioning structure that defines how the world works, so to speak.

> WAXMAN: In other words, you found that your view of the world, your ideology was not right, it was not working.

> GREENSPAN: Precisely. That is precisely the reason I was shocked, because I had been going for 40 years or more with very considerable evidence that this was working exceptionally well.[1]

---

1 US Congress, House Committee on Oversight and Government Reform (October 23, 2008).

What is called a worldview here can be easily understood as a basic assumption about how the world works. Such assumptions, which can also be about human nature or human relationships, are not easily changed. In fact, they are our reality, until some other reality confronts them. Our assumptions constitute our interpretations of the worlds in which we live.

Most of us live in multiple worlds, and we move among them without much difficulty. In fact, sometimes, their boundaries are very thin and they even overlap with each other. Still, we know the difference between a professional or business relationship and a family relationship. We know that there are different expectations among brothers and sisters than among co-workers. We may have some inkling of the difference between being a consumer and a citizen, but we may not know how to clearly express it.

So what are the assumptions (worldviews) behind the disagreement about whether work teams or their supervisors should decide how to get the work done? One way to figure this out is to think about what we would have to assume in order to agree with the different views. What would you have to assume about how things work in order to agree that work teams themselves should decide how to get their work done? Would you have to assume that there is some team spirit or camaraderie that provides the basis for dealing with any differences of opinion? Or would you have to assume that individuals in the team had similar notions of who is good at what? Conversely, what would you have to assume in order to agree that supervisors should have the authority to decide how work teams organize their work? Perhaps you would need to assume that most people, even in a team, will be more competitive than cooperative, and that they will never really agree on such issues.

One could explore these assumptions more and thus learn more about the worlds in which we live. Such an exploration not only increases our learning, but also enables us to become aware of what we have in common: what provides the basis for engaging in a conversation in the first place. If we continue the dialogue, in other words, we do so because of an unspoken agreement that allows us to explore our disagreements. As we shall see in the next chapter, this awareness of deeper agreements provides us with the possibility of engaging in an ethical analysis of our different positions.

Identifying Resources for Making Decisions

For now, we need to make sure we can identify the different elements of decision making: proposals, observations, value judgments, and assumptions. Worksheet 2-1 (see p. 33) will give you a chance to identify these four different types of resources for making good decisions. Once you have finished, you can discuss with others why you identified the sentences as you did.

When we examine the different types of sentences in this exercise, we can make several observations: Both proposals and value judgments express "should" statements. These are called normative statements because they express what we should or ought to do, in contrast to descriptive statements that express how things are. The difference between proposals and value judgments is that proposals are specific and value judgments are general. Observations also tend to be more specific than assumptions, but sometimes the observation is a general statement supported by empirical research.

So what can we do when someone questions any of these resources? If someone questions our proposals, we can share the reasons that support them—observations, values, and assumptions. To support our observations, we can point to empirical evidence. Value judgments, on the other hand, can be supported by connections with other values or even ethical theories. Assumptions are the most difficult to support, but we can show how they are coherent with other assumptions and are relevant to the issue at hand.

Skill in identifying these different resources will not always resolve disagreements, but it can eliminate a lot of confusion and frustration. If there is a disagreement about observations, for example, one can sometimes resolve it by collecting more data. But other times the relevant observations involve irresolvable uncertainties. The process of data collection may seem endless, and one might wonder why people keep repeating themselves. This may actually be a sign that the disagreement was not really about the facts (observations), but about something else, usually assumptions.

TABLE 2.2: STEPS INVOLVED IN SHARING RESOURCES		
State your position	**Proposal**	"Businesses should pay a carbon tax for their carbon emissions."
Support your proposal with your view of the facts	**Observation**	"A carbon tax will reflect the environmental costs of products, and the tax can be used to offset carbon emissions."
State why you believe this action is important and worthwhile	**Value Judgment**	"Consumers should know the environmental costs of products and we should offset carbon emissions."
Express the worldview that makes your argument relevant and feasible	**Assumption**	"I assume that people would rather know the true costs of things than be deceived."

One finds a similar confusion between proposals and value judgments. Sometimes people assume that if we share the same value judgment, such as individual freedom, we will also share the same proposal, such as the government should not require health care insurance. In fact, similar values may support very different proposals because of different assumptions. The ability to identify where we agree—such as similar values—and where we disagree—conflicting assumptions—will help us to focus not only on what divides us, but also on what unites us. Table 2.2 shows the steps involved in sharing our resources with others.

Moving from one step to another is not always as easy as it may appear, because we may not be aware of all the resources behind our proposals. In some cases, we may only be aware of our observations, not our value judgments and assumptions. A useful tool for discovering the implicit value judgments is the deductive syllogism, which is a logical structure or pattern of reasoning.

Creating Valid Syllogisms

We are going to use the syllogism in a special way: as a means of uncovering normative, rather than descriptive statements. We are interested, in other words, in syllogisms that support actions (proposals). Let's say I said, "We should eat breakfast every day (proposal), because studies have shown that a good breakfast is important for one's well being (observation)." What is the value judgment here? It is this: "We should do what is good for our well-being." This value judgment seems justifiable—it is praiseworthy and worthwhile—but how do I know it is the right value for this case? I can find out by using the rules of a valid syllogism.

Deductive syllogisms are argumentative structures that contain two premises or reasons and a conclusion. The structure of these elements is such that if the premises are true, the conclusion necessarily follows. Here is a standard deductive syllogism:

MAJOR PREMISE: *Humans are mortal.*
MINOR PREMISE: *Socrates is human.*
CONCLUSION: *Therefore, Socrates is mortal.*

An important rule for this type of syllogism is that the argument can have three and only three terms. The terms are called the minor term, the major term, and the middle term. The minor and major terms are in the conclusion and the middle term is in both premises. In this example, the minor term is Socrates, the major term is mortal and the middle term is human. The middle term, human, connects Socrates and mortal, because it is in both premises.

The syllogism about Socrates, of course, is not about action—not about what Socrates or anyone else should do. The basic rules of syllogisms, however, remain the same for action or "should" syllogisms as for traditional syllogisms. In syllogisms that support actions or proposals, there is also a middle term that is first expressed in the observation (the minor premise of the syllogism) and then repeated in the value judgment (the syllogism's major premise). The value judgment repeats the middle term introduced in the observation as a normative sentence, i.e., a sentence with a "should" verb.

> **VALUE JUDGMENT**: "We should increase our collective knowledge."
> **OBSERVATION**: "Diversity increases our collective knowledge."
> **PROPOSAL**: "We should maintain a diverse workforce."

The middle term here is "increase our collective knowledge," or some variation of this idea. Using this term in a normative sentence constitutes the logical value judgment. To use this process of spelling out an argument's value judgment, find the implicit value judgment of the arguments in Worksheet 2-2 (see p. 35).

To practice using the syllogism, select a controversial issue from your own experience or one that's in the news, and use Worksheet 2-3 (see p. 37) to develop syllogisms with proposals, observations, and value judgments.

After you have finished Worksheet 2-3, make sure that the observations can actually be verified by data and that the value judgments are "should" statements. Also, make sure that the value judgment repeats the middle term—the term that first appeared in the observation. If the syllogisms are valid, and the disagreement has not been resolved, then we need to go deeper to explore the source of the disagreement: the assumptions.

Exploring Assumptions

Remember that assumptions are our worldviews, our notions of how things work, and our view of human nature. In everyday life, we don't regard our worldview as an assumption, but as reality. In many cases, this "reality" becomes an assumption for us only when we encounter other realities—other assumptions. Because they are often taken-for-granted and quite deep, it is not easy to articulate them and to compare them with other assumptions. Still, this is the work before us if we want to learn from our disagreements.

Many different assumptions revolve around ways in which we see others as similar to us or as different. We are all humans, of course, but that may not have much traction in terms of our religious or cultural differences. On the other hand, many of us have similar responses to human tragedy wherever it occurs. One way to learn more about our assumptions about our similarities and differences is to engage in a dialogue with others about them. Worksheet 2-4 (see p. 39) provides an opportunity for such a dialogue. First write out your opinions about the similarities and differences among those in your group, and then share your answers with others and explore the similarities and differences in your answers.

In some cases, becoming aware of our assumptions about how we are similar and different may help us understand both why we disagree and how we might resolve the disagreement. For example, say one argues that women should not work as journalists in dangerous locations. If we have a chance to explore our assumptions about the similarities and differences between men and women, we might change our minds or at least have a better understanding of where we are coming from.

Sometimes, one can ask questions about the reasons for alternative views and figure out the assumptions of each side. Say you think corporations should be allowed to financially support political candidates and I do not. To understand the assumptions behind our arguments, I could ask, "What would I have to assume to agree with you?" This would lead me to imagine a worldview in which I could make an argument similar to yours (that corporations should be allowed to fund political candidates). If I assume that corporations are citizens like I am, then I would agree. That may not be your assumption, but if I did assume so, it would allow me to agree with you. Once I have developed this assumption, I can then use it to ask a second question: "Since I do not agree with you, what do I assume about the political status of corporations?" Or to put it another way, "If I don't assume they are citizens, what do I assume?" Well, maybe I assume they are the property of shareholders, and even though shareholders are citizens, their property is not. So now I know at least one assumption that others could have, and if they did, they would agree with me. If one assumed that citizens own corporations, then one would not propose that corporations should act as citizens. If one assumes, on the other hand, that corporations are like human citizens, then they should have the same rights as citizens. The basis for the disagreement is clear, and the issue is really quite thought provoking.

Another way to uncover assumptions is to imagine a world where you would change your mind. In this case, you use an imaginary world as a reflector to shed some light on the world you have taken for granted, that is, on your assumptions. Here one can say that I would change my mind if I assumed such and such a world, but since I do not assume that kind of world, I wonder what kind of world I do assume.

The purpose of these strategies for uncovering assumptions is to learn more about our own way of viewing the world than we knew before. A good way to begin is to acknowledge that we do not know what assumptions are relevant for the issue at hand. We learn this by stepping into the shoes of another or by imagining a different world. We then use these constructed assumptions as a way of reflecting back on our own. We learn about our assumptions, in other words, from people who differ from us or from situations that are different.

Stating our assumptions is not as easy as one might expect. Sometimes, one actually restates the observation or value judgment instead of going deeper to find the assumption. You want to make sure that assumptions express something new that is not already contained in the observations or value judgments. The sample argument in Table 2.3 begins with opposing proposals and ends with contrasting assumptions:

TABLE 2.3: SAMPLE ARGUMENT		
THE QUESTION	Should we seek corporate sponsors for university activities?	
	YOUR VIEW	**ALTERNATIVE VIEW**
PROPOSALS	*No, we should not.*	*Yes, we should.*
OBSERVATIONS	*They may limit the kinds of activities we can do.*	*We need the funds.*
VALUE JUDGMENTS	*We should not let corporations limit our university activities.*	*We should do what we need to do.*
ASSUMPTIONS	*I assume that whoever pays for something will ensure it does not have a negative impact on them.*	*I assume there is no other way to get the funds we need.*

Use Worksheet 2-5 (see p. 41) to see what assumptions come to mind with either the arguments you developed earlier or with new arguments. Try to imagine first what you would have to assume to agree with the alternative view, and then what you might have been assuming since you disagree with that view. Then try the second strategy. Imagine a world where you would hold a different person's view, and then from this vantage point, try to formulate the world you might have assumed to hold your actual view.

You can use Worksheet 2-6 (see p. 43) to further practice the methods presented in this chapter. First select a controversial issue and write out alternative proposals, and then identify the resources behind them—alternative observations, value judgments, and assumptions.

As we develop arguments for our alternative views, it may seem that we are returning to debate rather than dialogue. In fact, few identify arguing with dialogue, and yet that is what we are proposing here. We are moving toward the development of "argumentative dialogues," in which we join together in using the logic of arguments to understand and to share what we know with each other. This work includes not only exploring our observations, value judgments, and assumptions, but also evaluating them, which is the topic of the next chapter.

WORKSHEET 2-1   SORTING OUT DIFFERENT RESOURCES

Identify each of the following statements as a proposal (P), observation (O), value judgment (VJ), or assumption (A).

1   Businesses should use local vendors when they can.

2   Buying locally decreases carbon emissions.

3   We should promote sustainable communities.

4   No one gave business permission to harm the environment.

5   We treat everyone with respect.

6   Honesty is the best policy.

7   Most workers in the US do not have job security.

8   We should do what maximizes happiness.

9   The earth is slowly getting warmer.

10   We should support the development of public banks that are not driven by profit, but by service.

WORKSHEET 2-2   DISCOVERING IMPLICIT VALUE JUDGMENTS

EXAMPLES:

We should hire from within the company, because current employees understand the company culture.

VJ: We should hire people who understand our company culture.

Employees who receive health care benefits should not smoke, because smoking increases health care costs.

VJ: We should keep our health care costs as low as we can.

Corporations should not engage in political campaigns, because they are not really citizens.

VJ:

We should develop a strong core values statement, because employees will then know what we expect of them.

VJ:

We should let our daughter run the company, because she has good connections.

VJ:

We should support labor unions, because then workers will have a say in their work conditions.

VJ:

We should find a qualified minority candidate for the position, because they are underrepresented in our leadership team.

VJ:

We should locate our new factory in the city that gives us the best tax breaks, because that will help our bottom line.

VJ:

WORKSHEET 2-3   DEVELOPING VALID SYLLOGISMS

THE QUESTION

....

....

	Your View	*Alternative View*
PROPOSALS		
OBSERVATIONS		
VALUE JUDGMENTS		

WORKSHEET 2-4   ASSUMPTIONS ABOUT OURSELVES

How are we similar?	How are we different?
1	**1**
2	**2**
3	**3**
4	**4**
5	**5**

WORKSHEET 2-5   UNCOVERING ASSUMPTIONS

Alternative Views

P: _____

P: _____

O: _____

O: _____

VJ: _____

VJ: _____

Using Alternative Views to Discover Assumptions

To agree with the alternative view, I would have to assume that ...

To agree with the alternative view, I would have to assume that ...

Since I do not agree with the alternative view, I must assume that ...

Since I do not agree with the alternative view, I must assume that ...

Using Imagined Worlds to Discover Assumptions

I would change my mind if I imagined a world where ...

I would change my mind if I imagined a world where ...

Since I do not imagine that world, I must imagine a world where ...

Since I do not imagine that world, I must imagine a world where ...

WORKSHEET 2-6   DISCOVERING THE RESOURCES OF ALTERNATIVE VIEWS

THE QUESTION

	Your View	*Alternative View*
PROPOSALS		
OBSERVATIONS		
VALUE JUDGMENTS		
ASSUMPTIONS		

CHAPTER THREE

ENGAGING IN AN ETHICAL ANALYSIS OF HUMAN ACTION

Imagine this situation: We need to make a decision. We have carefully explored our different observations, value judgments, and assumptions. We realize why we support different proposals, but we still disagree about what to do. So what can we do now? We can shift gears from exploring to evaluating. We can shift the conversation to examining the merits of our different views by applying common ethical criteria to them that relate not only to our different worldviews but also to our common humanity. This does not mean that we escape our own worldviews, but rather that we see each worldview as one among others; as a result, even as we think from our own worldviews, we know that others from other worldviews join us in the conversation.

So I approach ethics from my particular worldview, and the ethical criteria used in this Workbook reflect that point of view. At the same time, my Western ethical framework has undergone significant changes in the past decades. Perhaps the most significant is the addition of a feminist perspective to what had been a male patriarchal worldview. Instead of focusing so much on the individual, isolated person, the feminist view has focused more on human relationships, and especially caring relationships.[1] One conclusion I have drawn from listening to a feminist

---

1 See Carol Gilligan, *In a Different Voice: Psychological Theory and Women's Development* (Cambridge, MA: Harvard University Press, 1982), and Virginia Held, *The Ethics of Care: Personal, Political, and Global* (New York: Oxford University Press, 2006).

ethics of care is that we always act in relationships and our acts have an impact on the relationships in our lives. We are relational beings, and the relationships that especially need our attention are caring relationships—parents caring for children, nurses caring for the sick, all of us caring for the elderly. How this consciousness changes our evaluation of different actions waits to be determined.

We are trying to figure out what is the best thing to do when we disagree and we both think we are right. To find the best course of action, we can apply ethical approaches to three central issues: (1) why we are doing something (our purpose), (2) what we are really doing (the principle behind our action), and (3) the impact of our action (the consequences). Let's name these three criteria an *ethics of purpose*, an *ethics of principle*, and an *ethics of consequence*. These three ethical approaches to issues correspond, somewhat, to different ways in which people tend to interpret moral questions. Let's call them the *moral visionary*, the *moral judge*, and the *moral assessor*.

The Visionary, the Judge, and the Assessor

The moral visionary says, "We have this vision of what we should do and of what kind of person or organization we should become, and we must do these things to realize our vision." Not everyone is a moral visionary, but we all probably do have aspirations for our lives, and an ethics of purpose shows how we can use them in making choices.

The typical saying of the moral judge is quite different from that of the moral visionary. It goes something like this: "You cannot do that because it is unfair and it violates human rights." The moral judge seeks to protect people's dignity. He or she allows only those actions that pass the test of the universal moral law. Keeping promises regardless of consequences is a good example; protecting human rights is another.

Instead of using one's aspirations to determine the right choice, the moral judge uses the rational principle of consistency.

The moral assessor also has a different voice. It may sound like this: "You need to consider the total impact of the proposed policy on others, before you can decide what to do." The moral assessor examines the consequences of different policies on selected groups and then assesses what policy will bring about the greater good. The greater good could be defined as the most pleasure or happiness, the maximization of value, or the satisfaction of preferences. In any case, the assessor uses the tools of comparison and contrast among different policies to determine which one is right.

We may find ourselves more comfortable in one role here than another, but most of us have some experience in all three types of moral reflection. Sorting them out and understanding their strengths and weaknesses will help us develop solutions to disagreements that will find support from various types of thinking, instead of just our own. This chapter will briefly explain these three ethical approaches and then outline how we can use them to evaluate the arguments we developed when exploring the observations, value judgments, and assumptions of alternative views.

The Ethics of Purpose

An ethics of purpose uses an agent's good purposes or worthy goals as standards to evaluate the merit of a particular action. Those actions are right that are in alignment with an agent's purposes. The Greek philosopher Aristotle is usually seen as the primary representative of this approach. His *Nicomachean Ethics* begins, "Every art and every investigation, and likewise every practical pursuit or undertaking, seems to aim at some good: hence it has been well said that the Good is that at which all things aim" (Book I: 1-3). Aristotle goes on to say that once we agree on what is good—what is worthwhile—then we can use it as a standard for selecting actions that are in alignment with it.

For Aristotle, our capacity to discern the good in any situation depends on our dispositions, or our virtues—such as courage or care. Closely connected with doing the right thing is being a good person. Ethics, in other words, includes both our actions and our character. We can capture these two dimensions of Aristotle's ethics by speaking of an agent's external purpose (action) and internal purpose (character).

Not everyone would agree with Aristotle that humans, as humans, have a purpose, but most would agree that if you want to achieve something, then you need to do those things that make it possible. Say you are considering whether or not to start your own business. Using this approach, you would first need to decide what kind of businessperson you want to be. What are the key virtues (internal purpose) of a good businessperson? Then you need to decide what you want your business to do well. What are the key goals (external purpose) of my business?

Not everything counts as a good purpose, of course, because some purposes might be realized through unethical means. Let's say you have the goal of piling up lots of money, and you are considering whether to take on a second job or to rob a bank. The goal of piling up lots of money doesn't help you discern which way of achieving that goal is ethically right. If the purpose is to serve as a standard for making good decisions, it must be valuable or worthwhile in itself. To apply an ethics of purpose, we need to agree on a worthwhile purpose, which we can then use to evaluate different courses of action.

Take the case of an accountant who is considering whether or not to work for a company that focuses more on profits than on reliable audits. From an ethics of purpose approach, the questions are as follows: What is a "good" accountant and "good" accounting? What should an accounting company strive for, and what should it become? Once we have these settled, a person can use this description to decide whether or not to take the job.

It is possible to apply an ethics of purpose to individuals and to organizations. As individuals, we can figure out—probably in conversations with others—the good we can achieve (external purpose) and the person we want to become (internal purpose). Once we have these goals or visions, we can use them to determine what we should do. For organizations, the good external purpose is quite similar to that of individuals: "What is the good purpose of the business?" The internal purpose, on the other hand, focuses on the character of the work community instead of the individual. It asks about the kind of work relationships one should strive to achieve. This is very close to an ethics of care.

An ethics of care reminds us that when making decisions we are deciding how we will honor our existing relationships as well as what kind of relationships we want to promote. Not all relationships are the same—e.g., family relationships may be quite different from work relationships—but even in work relationships we can decide to promote relationships of trust and respect or their opposite. Good relationships, in other words, can serve as the internal purpose of businesses and other organizations.

The Ethics of Principle

One can think of an ethics of purpose in terms of means and ends. The idea is to achieve an alignment between what one wants to achieve (the good end) and one's action (the right means). The ethics of principle frames issues quite differently. It ignores the end, instead examining the act by itself. Rather than using the good purpose to justify an action, this approach justifies an action by the principle of consistency.

The eighteenth-century philosopher Immanuel Kant is usually seen as the best representative of this ethical approach. Kant believed that the right thing to do was determined by obeying what he called the "Universal Moral Law." This law, however, was not dictated by any supreme being, but rather by human reason. As rational beings, we can rationally determine what kinds of actions are moral. That may seem dangerous, but here is Kant's reasoning. When we will an action, he believed we also, perhaps unconsciously, will a general principle that justifies it. An action is justifiable only if it conforms to a general principle that everyone should follow. This general principle is actually like the implicit value judgment we examined in the development of arguments in the last chapter. But Kant goes further than we did. He wants us to ask if that implicit principle or value judgment could become a universal moral law. Can it be applied in all similar cases? Can it be taken as a universal obligation? If so, then it is a moral law we must obey. For example, if you're wondering whether it's morally acceptable for you to leave work early just because you feel like it, you should ask whether it would be morally acceptable for everyone to leave work early just because they felt like it.

Furthermore, since we are the creators of the moral law, we should be treated as moral agents, which means with dignity. That also applies to all other persons as well. The right act, in other words, would be one whose implicit principle can become a universal moral law as well as one that respects the moral agency of others.

Say you are part of a management team considering how much your company could save in labor costs by changing some of its full-time positions to part-time ones. If these positions were for fewer than 20 hours per week, the company could save on benefits and could hire less experienced (and less expensive) people to take the jobs. Would an ethics of principle support such a policy? Well, what is the implicit principle operative here? Perhaps something like this: Those who control a business's workplaces should change the conditions of those workplaces when it is to the company's advantage to do so. Can you agree that they should be able to do this in all similar cases? And does this respect the moral agency of others, especially the workers? These are the questions that would need positive answers before you would find support for this policy from an ethics of principle.

Kantian ethics is sometimes taken as the epitome of an individualistic ethics, since its focus is on human freedom and individual choice, regardless of consequences. It appears that there is not much concern for caring relationships in this approach. From this perspective, one should tell the truth, for example, regardless of its impact on others. In some cases, this may seem morally wrong, but that does not mean we should ignore this approach. It means instead that we need the other two—ethics of purpose and ethics of consequence—to increase our chances of doing the right thing. In fact, each approach has its own weaknesses and needs the others to correct them.

Of the three ethical approaches in this Workbook, the ethics of principle most clearly aligns itself with modern notions of justice and human rights. The notion of consistency lies behind most views of justice, which is that of treating equals equally and treating unequals unequally. The question, of course, is how we identify who is equal and who is unequal. On the one hand, we can say that we are all equal and therefore deserve equal treatment. This is the area of human rights. All humans have the same rights, because they are moral agents and because we share a common humanity. On the other hand, we are also unequal—or rather different—in various respects, and therefore we deserve unequal or different treatment, which is the area of distributive justice. Distributive justice addresses questions of how different kinds of goods should be fairly distributed. Bonuses at work, for example, might be distributed according to the employees' contributions to the business; health care benefits might be distributed by people's need for health care. The point is that different goods may have different criteria for a fair distribution. Table 3.1 defines some of the most commonly used criteria for deciding how things should be distributed.

TABLE 3.1: PRINCIPLES OF DISTRIBUTIVE JUSTICE	
Equality	Each one receives the same
Need	Those who need more receive more
Contribution	Those who contribute more receive more
Usefulness	Those who can make better use of a good receive more
Status	Those who belong to certain groups receive more
Fair procedure	Who gets what depends on a fair process

In contrast to an ethics of purpose, where one strives to achieve some good goal, principles of human rights and justice are mostly principles that one strives not to violate. At least that is one way of using rights and justice as criteria for making good decisions. If one were thinking of monitoring an employee's email, for example, one question would be whether or not that violates a person's right to privacy. Or if one distributes promotions based on good looks, we need to ask if that violates the principle of justice that should be used in the distribution of promotions. A morally right act follows not only what we should do, but also what we should not do.

The Ethics of Consequence

In contrast to the ethics of purpose that begins with describing the good purpose of the actor, or the ethics of principle that focuses on the act itself, an ethics of consequence ignores both the actor's aspirations and an act's implicit principle. Instead it focuses on the impact of the act upon all those it affects. The right thing to do is what has the most positive consequences overall. This ethical approach has its origin in eighteenth-century utilitarianism.

Jeremy Bentham is usually recognized as the father of utilitarianism. He belonged to a British tradition that was much more empirical and pragmatic than the German philosophy of Kant. Bentham thought that right and wrong could be determined by measuring the pleasure and pain they brought on others. He called this a "moral calculus." This might seem value-free, since one only has to measure the consequences of an action. The problem, however, is how to select the correct measuring stick. Bentham thought it was pleasure and pain. For him, pleasure was happiness, so he coined the slogan for his utilitarianism thus: "The greatest happiness for the greatest number." The philosopher John Stuart Mill, who followed in Bentham's footsteps, believed it was not just the quantity of happiness, but also the quality.

Whether one uses pleasure or pain, or some other good and bad to measure consequences, this approach helps us to determine the best decision by comparing the consequences of alternative proposals. Instead of evaluating an action in terms of its alignment with one's aspirations, this approach compares and contrasts the probable impact that alternative courses of action will have in the real world.

A case where one can save multiple lives by sacrificing just one is a common way of illustrating this approach. The choices are either to sacrifice one and save several, or not to sacrifice one and let the several perish. If one thinks only of immediate consequences, sacrificing the one may seem right. If one considers long-term consequences, on the other hand, the answer may not be so clear. What is clear is that this approach needs both an ethics of purpose and an ethics of principle to improve the chances of not making a moral mistake.

If one sees the ethics of consequence as a careful examination of the impact of one's decision on others, it seems to fit easily with an ethics of care, especially if it includes an action's impact on relationships as well as on persons. At the same time, this approach has little space for either justice or human rights, since both could be trumped if one gets better consequences by violating rights and principles of justice. To ensure the responsible use of this approach, one needs to be careful in selecting the groups that will be impacted, because including or excluding a group will change the total positive and negative consequences.

We can use all three ethical approaches to think about corporate social responsibility (CSR). An ethics of consequence would interpret CSR as taking into account the impact of corporate decisions on both their stakeholders—those groups that have a stake in corporate decisions—and the natural environment. CSR can also be supported by an ethics of principle in terms of the principle of respect for different stakeholders and the planet. Even an ethics of purpose could support CSR in terms of the question of what kind of business one wants to create and maintain. Without a strong sense of a business's purpose, it actually seems rather strange to decide what one should do (one's responsibilities) without knowing why one exists in the first place. In any case, all three approaches can provide a stronger justification for CSR than any one by itself. This is true, as well, when we apply these three ethical approaches to evaluate our arguments on controversial issues.

Worksheets 3-1 to 3-3 (see pp. 59-63) provide a step-by-step process of applying the ethical approaches to the arguments developed by using the worksheets in the previous chapter. By examining the value judgments within your arguments, you might find that they match one of the three approaches more than the others. A value judgment that expresses one's aspirations or a company's purpose would match an ethics of purpose. A value judgment that relates to justice or fairness might be closer to an ethics of principle. And a value judgment that expresses the type of consequences one values, such as increased safety, would employ an ethics of consequence.

So in applying the three ethical approaches to evaluate your arguments, you may find that your argument is closer to one approach than the others. You can begin with that approach and then work through the others. The strongest argument will have support from all three approaches. This does not mean, of course, that everyone will now agree. In fact, you may feel that the inquiry has resulted in more support for your position. Still, there may also be some agreements you can use to move forward. By holding together the agreements and disagreements, you may be able to develop new or modified proposals that take into account all that you have learned in the process.

Applying an Ethics of Purpose

An ethics of purpose uses the agent's *good* purpose for evaluating alternative agruments. The agent is usually the one making the decision, or it could be the organization that will implement it. If a proposal promotes the agent's good purpose(s), then it is the right thing to do, according to this ethical approach.

Agents have both external and internal purposes, as discussed previously. For example, an individual's external purpose may be to realize a special talent and her internal purpose may be to act with integrity. A firm may have the external purpose of producing good toys and the internal purpose of developing a good work community.

Applying an Ethics of Principle

An ethics of principle begins by stating the implicit principle of the proposed actions, which may be an argument's value judgment. The key question is whether this principle could become a universal moral law.

Also, since this approach relies on our capacity as moral agents, we need to ensure that it respects the moral agency of others and does not violate human rights or principles of justice.

Applying an Ethics of Consequence

An ethics of consequence evaluates different proposals in terms of the balance of their positive and negative consequences on the groups that are impacted. The proposal that does the most good and the least harm would be the right thing to do, according to this approach. Selecting who will be included in the analysis is crucial.

Developing the Modified Proposal

In some cases, an ethical evaluation of all the competing arguments will resolve the disagreement by showing that one argument has more strengths than the others. In other cases, even though the parties understand the reasons for and the merits of their positions, they will continue to disagree. When disagreement remains, the participants can usually take advantage of what they have learned from each other by using the strengths of the alternative arguments to modify their original positions.

Remember the case about who should decide how a work team gets its work done? Let's see what happens when we apply the three ethical approaches. An ethics of purpose asks about the external and internal purpose. Since we don't know what this team contributes to the company or community, the question of the external purpose cannot be clearly answered. We can say, however, that the team has some goal it wants to achieve, and then we can ask if more autonomy or less autonomy fits with that goal. There doesn't seem to be a clear answer. The application of the internal purpose may help us more. What kind of team do we want to promote? Do we want a team where people realize their fullest potential as creative workers? If so, then not letting them decide how to organize their work might prevent them from actually becoming the best they can be.

What about an ethics of principle? What is the implicit principle of each proposal? One seems to be that we should promote group harmony. Can we make that a universal moral law? Should we always promote group harmony? What about the implicit principle of the other proposal? Should we always give people a say in how they work together? And a related question: Which proposal respects the moral autonomy of the team members more? And what about human rights and justice? What is being distributed here? Work. How should it be distributed? Perhaps by a person's capacity to do the work or usefulness. And who knows their capacity better than the worker or team of workers? If work should be distributed by usefulness, then perhaps it is the workers themselves who know best what they are useful for. From the perspective of an ethics of principle, it seems that the better proposal is the one that gives the team more autonomy.

So what are the probable consequences of each proposal for the groups that will be impacted by our decision? The first group is the team. Other teams may also be affected as well as the whole company. If the impact on the company is greater than the impact on the team, then the right thing to do will probably be determined by its impact on company performance. Let's say that the probable consequences slightly favor maintaining group harmony. The question then is if the consequences are large enough to override the support for team autonomy from an ethics of principle and the open question of what kind of work community we want to promote. For me, when I look at the conclusions from all three ethical approaches, the promotion of team autonomy has a slight advantage. Still, in order to take advantage of this choice, we can modify our proposal to include the concern for group harmony. Let's say that we should let teams decide how to allocate their workload among themselves as long as all members get some training in dealing with disagreement, so they have the capacity to have good conversations about how to work together.

In many cases, when people disagree, applying the three ethical approaches will give some support to different proposals. By applying all three, we can recognize the strengths of different views, and usually come to a conclusion about what is the best thing to do when we both think we are right.

We have been imagining how to deal with disagreement on important questions at work: how to examine our different observations, value judgments, and assumptions, and then how to evaluate our arguments by an ethics of purpose, principle, and consequence. Now we are ready to move from imagination to action, or at least to deliberation about the best course of action. Making all of this work is the topic of the next chapter.

WORKSHEET 3-1   APPLYING AN ETHICS OF PURPOSE

Agent/Actor

Agent's Good External and Internal Purposes/Aspirations

Which proposal best promotes the agent's aspirations?

Which proposal best promotes good relationships?

WORKSHEET 3-2   APPLYING AN ETHICS OF PRINCIPLE

Alternative Proposals	Alternative Implicit Principles

Which implicit principle can become a Universal Moral Law and respects the dignity of others?

Does either proposal violate principles of justice or human rights?

WORKSHEET 3-3   APPLYING AN ETHICS OF CONSEQUENCE

Key persons/things impacted by the decision

**Positive and Negative Consequences
of First Proposal**

**Positive and Negative Consequences
of Second Proposal**

Which proposal will deliver the best consequences for all?

CHAPTER FOUR

DOING THE WORK

Like any process or method, the process of argumentative dialogues looks fairly easy in the abstract. Just use the syllogism to develop the arguments on each side, explore the different assumptions, and then evaluate the acquired knowledge with the three ethical approaches. But the devil, as they say, is in the detail. Engaging in a dialogue is not that easy when we really believe we are right and others are wrong, especially when it seems as if they refuse to listen to the persuasiveness of our views.

Sometimes, such as in a classroom or other educational setting, we can acknowledge that we are "offline," so to speak, which could give us permission to suspend our positions for a moment and really consider the merits of different views. In other situations, we seem to be "online," and there is no way we want to pretend that other views deserve the same consideration as ours. In such situations, we cannot use the process of argumentative dialogue in the same way as we can in the classroom, but we can use the process to clarify the arguments supporting different points of view.

Working Offline

Written assignments: When reading about controversial issues, one usually comes across some stated reasons for supporting different opinions, but other reasons remain implicit. In many cases, one never learns about the underlying assumptions. To understand and assess these diverse opinions on controversial issues, one can use the argumentative structure of the syllogism to gain a fuller understanding of the reasons behind them as well as to analyze their merit in terms of different ethical criteria—purpose, principle, and consequence.

Class Discussions: Argumentative dialogues are really designed for live conversations about controversial issues. In learning to use the process, students can move into small groups and use the process to explore their views on different issues.

Class Presentations: Argumentative dialogues can also serve as a method for structuring student presentations. Worksheet 4-1 (see p. 77) may serve as a template for developing the resources. More about this later.

Working Online

In contrast to the classroom, where all participants in a conversation can use the same process to explore and evaluate different views, many of our conversations occur with people whose arguments are not sorted out as the process indicates. So how can we use this method with them? It depends. In some situations, it may be impossible. The process does depend on some agreement—perhaps assumptions about our common humanity. If these agreements do not exist, then the likelihood of a good conversation on controversial issues is rather remote. At the same time, if we can talk about what we do share, the underlying agreements may emerge through the conversation.

The point is that analyzing and evaluating the reasons behind each other's position requires mutual consent. Once these conditions are met, then it is possible to clarify each other's arguments and to evaluate them.

Even when others do not know the different aspects of the process, it can be used to help clarify thinking. Here are some tips:

1. Try to distinguish between observations and assumptions.
2. Ask about the evidence for observations.
3. Ask what one would have to assume to change one's mind.
4. Express the implicit value judgment that fits with the arguments.
5. Suggest other values—such as justice or human rights— that might help to expand the conversation.

The possibility of using the process of argumentative dialogues to improve mutual understanding and policy formation finally rests on the quality of the dialogue that the participants are able to generate. A good dialogue will include listening, questioning, reflection, and learning. This can happen in any setting where people invite each other to a common endeavor to work through their disagreements.

Developing Argumentative Dialogues

You can use Worksheet 4-1 (see p. 77) to develop your outline for argumentative dialogues. Its purpose is to provide a means for integrating all the material that you will have developed by doing the worksheets in earlier chapters. The whole process includes both the analysis of different arguments and the ethical evaluation of them. So before you fill in this worksheet, you will want to use the worksheets in Chapters 2 and 3, and then transfer what you have learned to this worksheet.

In selecting the best course of action, all participants should consider the strengths of each point of view, as well as what they have learned from each other, and create a proposed course of action that takes this into account. Participants may agree to disagree, or they may see how one could develop a stronger proposal by letting the strengths of one view serve as a condition or limit on the other. The purpose of argumentative dialogues is to facilitate a good dialogue in which the participants engage in a critical and creative conversation.

A Sample Argumentative Dialogue on Worker Cooperatives

TONI: When I expand my business, I plan on making it a worker cooperative.

RY: You want to do what?

TONI: As my business grows, I want to bring on new people as co-owners of the business.

RY: You mean you want to give away the business to others?

TONI: No, I want to build the business with others who share the risks and the rewards of running a business.

RY: Well, I think that is a bad idea. I think you should maintain ownership of the business and hire people when you need them, and be able to fire them when you don't.

TONI: So you don't think we should share ownership?

RY: Never, and I will tell you why. We should not because that would mean giving up control of the business and we should maintain control.

TONI: Well, at least your argument is valid.

RY: What do you mean?

TONI: It's a good syllogism, with an observation and value judgment supporting your proposal.

RY: OK, so do you agree with it?

TONI: No, I disagree with your value judgment. I think we should share control with those whose fate is tied up in the direction of the business. I think we should design businesses as worker cooperatives because then everyone working in the business will have some say in the direction of the business and I think we all should have a say in decisions that can seriously affect our lives.

RY: Good logical argument.

TONI: Thanks.

RY: Have you done any research on this?

TONI: Yes, there are over 300 worker coops in the United States, in various industries from food to home care. The biggest worker coop is Mondragon in Spain. This cooperative conglomerate owns $33.5 billion in assets and employs more than 92,000 workers, many of whom are owners of the group. There are plenty of examples of successful worker cooperatives.

RY: Well, for me to agree with you, I would have to assume that I would get more enjoyment working with others, than I would get from having others work for me. Don't you want to be a captain of your own ship? I see myself as an entrepreneur, and I hope a very successful one.

TONI: Yes, I guess I do assume that working on a team would be more satisfying for me. We may be quite different on this score. But it's not only about me. I assume that many have similar aspirations as I do, and I really don't want to put myself in a position of controlling them or them controlling me. I assume that we don't have to design a business with a military command and control structure. We could be more like a soccer team.

RY: I don't know of any soccer teams that are worker cooperatives.

TONI: True, I was referring to how they all contribute to the success of their team. When you think about it, I don't see why players should not own their teams. If you were a soccer player would you like to have a say in decisions that affect you and your team?

RY: Sure, but that's not how things are done, especially in professional sports. Players go to the highest bidder. They go where someone will pay them to play.

TONI: I am not suggesting that we take on the powerful institutions of professional sports. I simply wanted to use the players' teamwork to illustrate what a worker coop could achieve, and what I would like to try.

RY: OK, but you must realize that most players engage in cooperative teamwork because they are motivated by money and fear of losing their position to the player waiting on the bench.

TONI: Don't you think lots of players really like playing the game and playing it well?

RY: That may be true of a few, but if they don't watch their back, they will not be playing very long.

TONI: We seem to have very different assumptions here. If I assumed that the only way to get people to excel is through incentives or punishments, then I would agree that co-ownership would be unwise. But I assume that many people are more or less like me. We want to have some control over our work and we want to do well.

RY: Well, I think a lot of people just want a paycheck, and are happy to have a job.

TONI: We really do have different assumptions.

RY: So it seems. You appear to focus more on the importance of good relationships and maybe I focus more on individual achievement, but both are important.

TONI: Yes, I agree, we need to find some balance between them. Perhaps we can do this by evaluating the ethical strength of the different arguments we have developed.

RY: OK, where should we start?

TONI: We can start with my first argument about what kind of business I want to run. One ethical question that relates to this argument is the question of what a good business would look like. What is its purpose?

RY: And what would you say?

TONI: Well I think a good business meets some needs and wants of the people in its community. I see businesses as providers of goods and services, and a good business would do that well.

RY: OK, but I don't think you have to be a worker-owned cooperative to provide excellent goods and services.

TONI: I agree, but I also want to create an excellent community of people who together provide these goods and services: this is really a business's internal purpose. I think the work community should be one of mutual respect and responsibility, and a worker cooperative is a good way to become that kind of business.

RY: Well, I can see that in an ideal world, but you may not realize your external purpose if you focus too much on your internal purpose. You know what I mean?

TONI: Yes, I know we have to make it in the market, but as I have said before, worker coops have been quite successful.

RY: Let's look at my argument from an ethics of principle.

TONI: Great. What is your implicit principle? It is probably the same as your argument's value judgment. Can you make that into a universal moral law?

RY: The value judgment was: "Owners should maintain control of their business." I guess I can re-word it to say something like "People should not give up control of things they own."

TONI: OK, this is a bit complicated, since we are thinking about whether or not to share ownership. It doesn't seem like it is morally wrong to share ownership, but then at the same time, it doesn't seem like we have a moral obligation to share something we own. I guess we need to know what you actually own when you own a business.

RY: Well, you own the assets, and you own the income it generates. You own the profit.

TONI: You may own the financial capital and the material capital, but you do not own the social or cultural capital—the human capital. You might pay for them, but you do not own them. If there are parts of every business that you do not own, then why should you control those parts?

RY: OK. You know, it doesn't seem that the ethics of principle really helps us evaluate the merit of my argument.

TONI: I think you are right. Not all three ethical approaches are equally helpful in every case. That may be true in this case in terms of trying to universalize the implicit principle, but what about the second question we ask when using this approach: "Does your proposal respect the moral agency of others?"

RY: Good question. As much as I hate to admit it, your position that people should have a say in decisions that affects them shows more respect for others than mine does. I think we need to move on to an ethics of consequence.

TONI: Fine with me. Who will be affected by our decision?

RY: You will be, or whoever is sharing ownership with those who join the business. Let's call them workers. Then we have your family and the other workers' families. We should include the other relevant stakeholders as well, such as the consumers, investors, the community, and suppliers.

TONI: And what do you see as the impact on these different groups? And do you think it will be positive or negative?

RY: For you, or whoever wants to share ownership of a business, the positive consequence would be that you would have company (no pun intended), but the negative is that, from my perspective, you increase the risk of failure. The workers might gain, if the business goes well, or lose, if it does not. I don't think the other stakeholders would be affected much.

TONI: What about the community? If the business is owned by a group of people who live in the community, isn't it more likely that the business will be responsive to its community? Furthermore, I think that since worker cooperatives promote active involvement at work, they will also promote more active involvement in other communities, such as public schools.

RY: Could be. Once I think more about this, the real issue seems to be the competitors. If your worker-cooperative is not competitive, the whole business will fail. That would be a negative consequence for everyone, including the community.

TONI: Right, I think we are dealing with risk and safety here, and if we take care when adding co-owners as we grow, I think the consequences can be quite positive for most of us.

RY: OK, if you are willing to take the risk. Also, if we look at our application of the three ethical approaches, it certainly does not rule out moving toward worker-cooperatives, so I would have to say it seems like a sound decision.

TONI: Yes, but I think I need to be careful in adding new owners, so maybe you would like to give me some feedback when the time comes. Hey, would you like to be the first co-owner?

RY: I don't think I am ready right now. Working with someone like you, however, would not be a bad idea.

TONI: Let's keep in touch.

WORKSHEET 4-1   AN OUTLINE FOR YOUR ARGUMENTATIVE DIALOGUES

THE QUESTION

	Your View	*Alternative View*
The syllogisms: proposal, observation, and value judgment for each view (use worksheets in Chapter 2)		
The underlying assumptions of each syllogism (use worksheets in Chapter 2)		

Evaluation (use worksheets in Chapter 3)

ETHICS OF PURPOSE

ETHICS OF PRINCIPLE

ETHICS OF CONSEQUENCE

BEST DECISION

GLOSSARY

ARGUMENT   A logical structure of propositions where conclusions are supported by reasons.

ASSUMPTIONS   Worldviews of how things fit together. Usually taken for granted until questioned by others.

DEBATE   A contest to test the strengths and weaknesses of different proposals.

DIALOGUE   A joint endeavor to understand each other's position through mutual inquiry and reflection.

DISAGREEMENT   Conflicting views of the right thing to do based on different observations, values, and assumptions.

ETHICS OF CONSEQUENCE   Focuses on the impact or consequences of different proposals on those who are affected by the decision.

ETHICS OF PRINCIPLE   Examines whether the implicit principle of an action can become a moral law for all to follow, and whether it conforms to our understanding of justice.

ETHICS OF PURPOSE   Examines whether the action promotes or aligns with the good purpose of the agent or actor.

NORMATIVE STATEMENTS   Statements that express what "should" be
rather than what "is."

OBSERVATIONS   The "facts" or data that can either be verified by
empirical research or justified by other reliable data.

PROPOSALS   Positions on controversial issues that express one's conclusions drawn from observations, values, and assumptions.

SYLLOGISM   An argumentative form that depends on the structure of
reasons and conclusions to justify one's position.

VALUE JUDGMENTS   Beliefs about what is worthwhile and praiseworthy that support decisions about actions.

from the publisher

A name never says it all, but the word "broadview" expresses a good deal of the philosophy behind our company. We are open to a broad range of academic approaches and political viewpoints. We pay attention to the broad impact book publishing and book printing has in the wider world; we began using recycled stock more than a decade ago, and for some years now we have used 100% recycled paper for most titles. As a Canadian-based company we naturally publish a number of titles with a Canadian emphasis, but our publishing program overall is internationally oriented and broad-ranging. Our individual titles often appeal to a broad readership too; many are of interest as much to general readers as to academics and students.

Founded in 1985, Broadview remains a fully independent company owned by its shareholders—not an imprint or subsidiary of a larger multinational.

If you would like to find out more about Broadview and about the books we publish, please visit us at **www.broadviewpress.com**. And if you'd like to place an order through the site, we'd like to show our appreciation by extending a special discount to you: by entering the code below you will receive a 20% discount on purchases made through the Broadview website.

Discount code: **broadview20%**

Thank you for choosing Broadview.

Please note: this offer applies only to sales of bound books within the United States or Canada.

The interior of this book is printed on 100% recycled paper.